Bodmin Building Hotels & Inns

by

Bill Johnson & Peter Davies

Published by Bodmin Town Museum, Mount Folly, Bodmin, Cornwall, PL31 2HQ

We would like to thank the following people and organisations:

The volunteers at Bodmin Town Museum, for access to documents, maps and photographs. The Cornish Studies Library, Redruth, for permission to use photographs from the *'Ellis Collection'*, the Cornwall Records Office for supplying documents, the Courtney Library, Truro for access to the '1822 Street Plan of Bodmin', 'The Cornwall Online Census Project' for census and Parish Records data, 'Historical Directories', University of Leicester, and Dudley Prout, Malcolm McCarthy, Joan Butler, Clemens of Bodmin and Mrs Sandoe for permission to use images and documents.

The unmarked historical images are from the collections of Bodmin Town Museum and the authors. Modern images are the Copyright of J M Johnson.   W H Johnson & P J C Davies,   April, 2012

Cover: Edited image of 'Sandoe's Royal Hotel' by Mardon's of Bristol (before 1900).

© **William Henry Johnson & Peter John Cule Davies, 2012**

All rights reserved. No part of this publication may be reproduced, stored in a retrieval system, or transmitted in any form or by any means electrical, mechanical, photocopied, recorded or otherwise, without prior permission of the authors.

Published by:
Bodmin Town Museum, Mount Folly, Bodmin, Cornwall, PL31 2HQ.
Manuscript prepared for publication by W H & J M Johnson, the publishing team.
ISBN 978-0-9570642-1-8
Printed by Mid Cornwall Printing, Truro, Cornwall

Introduction

Some history of the hotels and inns of Bodmin has been published in *'Old Cornish Inns'* by H L Douch[1] and *'Inn Signs'* an essay by L E Long[2]. This new work uses both these earlier books and the references cited therein, together with Directories (1791-1939),[3] Census Data (1831-1911),[4] the street plan of ca.1822 (Courtney Library, Truro),[5] the Tithe Map (published 1841) with the related Apportionment details (1840),[6] the OS maps of 1881 and 1907,[7] the Malcolm McCarthy Collection[8] and the National Archives (a2a database).[9]

The articles on hotels and inns are arranged alphabetically. In cases where different inns have been on the same plot, the oldest name appears first in the title.

A full index of hotel and inn names is included on page 47.

There are a number of signs mentioned in both Douch[1] and Long[2] and in other documents which are single entries. This could be because there are few records for the establishment; the name lasted a very short time; it was not an inn or hotel, that is, it did not provide food and accommodation for travellers or it was just a beer-house. John Burton refers to these beer-houses as *Kiddleywinks* o*r Kibby's*.

Beer-houses: Wallis reported seven beer houses in the Census of 1831. He later published changes to these businesses between the 30th May 1831 (Census Day) and 12th December 1831: *Colly* and *Harper* had closed their houses in Prison lane and the *Miner's Arms*, Higher Bore Street was closed. Harris had just opened a new house in Lower Bore Street.

This data shows the transient nature of the beer houses. Of the seven mentioned, two had closed and a new one opened in just a few months. Other examples have been found in later documents. However two beer-houses were not transient as they still exist in Bodmin in 2012!

A list of inns and beer-houses which are mentioned only once or twice and for which no further information has been found is included on page 45.

The Early Street Plan (1822)

A document lodged with the Courtney Library, Truro by Rev. William Iago in the late 1890s, (RIC, MMP/22/1.), is a hand-coloured street plan of Bodmin town from about 1822. Each property is clearly marked with a number. The inns and hotels are marked with their names.

From a study of this document, it is possible to position each of these buildings onto the street plan taken from the Tithe Map of 1840. A few street names were different in 1822. For example Carriers lane (Market Street) and Back St (Pool St). The 'main street' consisted of Fore Street and Bore Street.

The numbering system for Fore St started with the property on the corner between Prison Lane and Honey St (No.1), and continued westward up to 40. This means that the **Bell Inn** was 'behind 13 Fore Street' & the **Mason's Arms** was 14. 41 was on the south side of the street and the numbers increased eastwards. The **Red Lion** was 57 and **The Queen's Head** was 83. The same system was used for Bore Street. North side Nos.1-66 and south side started at 67. The **Garland Ox** was 63 and the **White Hart** was 110, next door to 41, Fore Street.

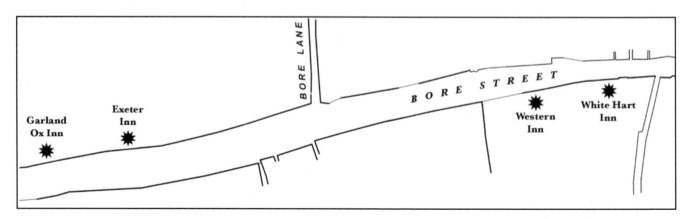

The street plan identifies the names and positions of twenty inns & hotels in Bodmin. The Pigot's Directory of Cornwall for 1823/4 lists nineteen with their keepers. The missing entry is for the **Golden Lion**. Together they give a good data set for the town but they do not cover villages in the Borough.

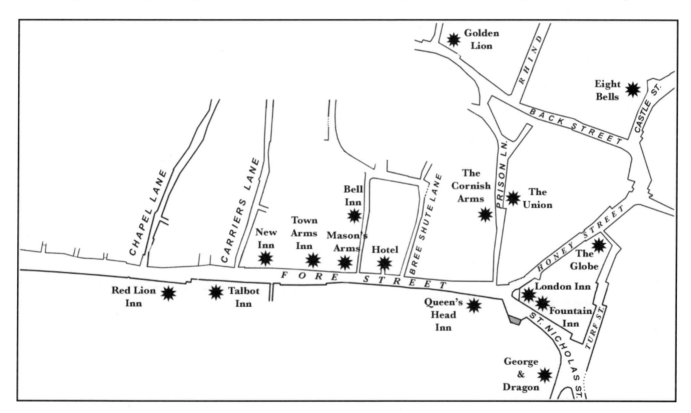

Tithe Map (1841)

The adjacent plans show the position of 23 of the 25 inns & hotels reported in the Tithe Map of 1841. **The Borough Arms** at Dunmeer is not shown and the entry for the **Miners Arms** at St Lawrence just shows the occupier as 'Truro Infirmary' but the inn is recorded in the 1841 Census.

There are three new signs; **The Spry; Barley Sheaf** and the **Omnibus**. The **Mason's Arms** has moved and the **White Hart** is not present.

In the following discussion of the various individual Hotels & Inns their positions will be identified by their Tithe Map plot numbers. This same number will be used as an identifier on later maps and census entries.

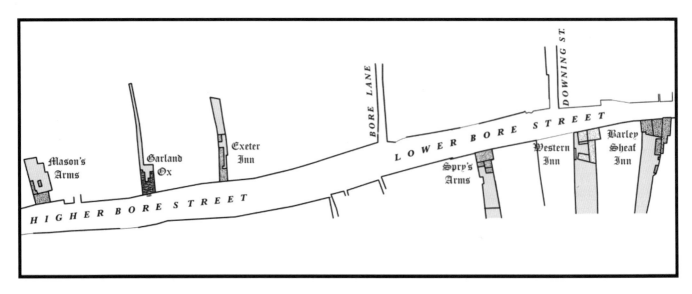

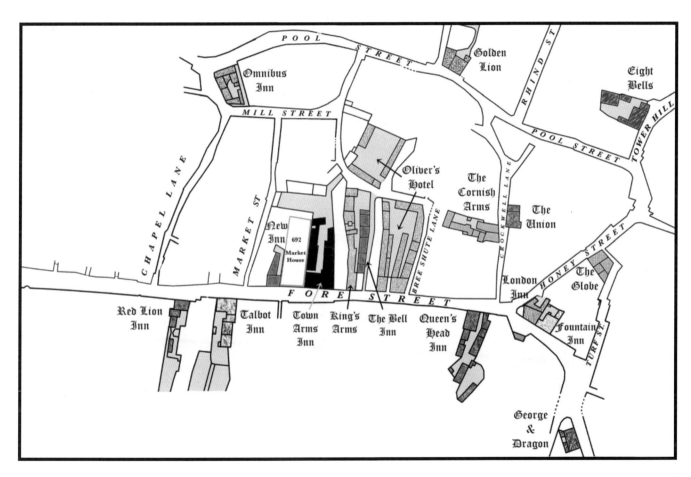

Bell Inn (Plot 704)

The **Bell Inn** was listed in 1791 in Bell Lane (Bell Lane was private and belonged to the inn) with occupier Mary Ann Carpenter. In the 1820s and early 1830s, the keepers were Jas. Coul and Eyre.

Before 1839 the house was taken over by Charles Phillipps, who was keeper until his death in 1857. His wife continued the business until her death in 1863. There are no further records for this inn.

Site of Inn (2012): Western side of Bell Lane behind 29, Fore Street, 'Dorothy Perkins'.

Entrance to Bell Lane from Fore Street | Bell Lane: Buildings on right site of Bell Inn | Entrance to Bell Lane from Fore Street (2012)

Blue Hart / Eight Bells (Plot 58)

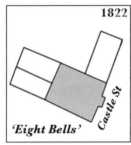
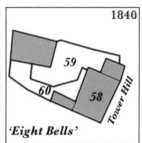

A sale document in the Malcolm McCarthy Collection, dated 6th July 1808, between Nicholas Wallis Penrose and John Colwell his Heirs and Assigns states: *"that Dwelling House situate lying and being within the said Borough of Bodmin in a certain Street there called Castle Street otherwise Tower Hill Street which said Dwelling House has for many years past been used as an Alehouse or Public House and till lately was called or known by the name of the **Blue Hart** and is now known by the name of the **Eight Bells** and is now in the occupation of Thomas Richards"*.

The **Blue Hart** is listed in the 1790s Directories and the **Eight Bells Inn** is on the 1822 plan. In 1822-3 and 1831, the occupier was James Bennett, and in 1839 John Kingsland. In 1840 the landowner was Julia Cavell and the occupier William Cavell. The last recorded entry for this Inn was in 1847. (The closure and sale was related to events in the Cavell family. For details see the *George & Dragon* section.) *Site of Inn (2012): 2 & 4, Castle Street.*

The Board / Hole in the Wall (Plot 748)

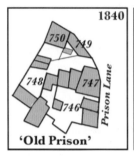

This is the site of the Debtors Prison which closed in 1779. By 1841 this site was known as the 'Old Prison' and was occupied by nine households including John Crang, a 20 year old writer. Before 1851 he had opened a Wine & Spirit Merchant business in Crockwell Street. In 1873 he was described as *'Importer of Wines & Spirits, Ale and Porter, Wholesale and retail wine, spirit and hop merchant'*. The premises were fully licensed and known as **The Board.**

John Crang, who was Mayor of Bodmin in 1871 & 1874-6, died in 1881 aged 62. In 1883 the business was owned by William Coppin Wickett & Co. He was a wine & spirit merchant of Redruth. His wife was Caroline Williams Crang and his son was named William Crang Wickett. It seems that he had inherited the business from the late John Crang.

Before 1889 the Wine & Spirit business was owned by Redruth Brewery. The branch manager was James Andrew Jane until his death in 1897 when he was replaced by his son John Charles Jane. Before 1914 Redruth Brewery had moved from Crockwell Street to the premises known as *'The Globe'* in Honey Street and John Charles Jane (J C Jane & Co.) became the new owner of 16 Crockwell Street. Also in 1914 there was a challenge to the licence on the grounds that the licensed premises were situated at the bottom of a yard, that there was no accommodation for man other than drinking purposes and there was no accommodation for horses or traps. Mr Jane stated that only 10% of his retail customers drank on the premises and that the majority ordered products to be delivered to their homes. As there were no other reports of problems, the licence was renewed.[10] Although these premises were licensed for many years, the sign of the **Hole in the Wall** did not appear until after the death of J C Jane in 1940. The 'Hole in the Wall' visitors' books from 1941 to 1984 are held by Bodmin Town Museum.

The **Hole in the Wall** is still open today.

Borough Arms, Dunmeer (Plot 1945)

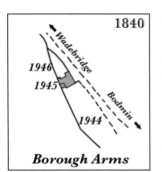

On the St Austell Brewery website it states that the **Borough Arms** (also known as the '**Borough Bounds**') was built in 1851 for railway workers moving china clay from the moor to Padstow. In fact this inn was recorded in the 1831 census and is probably older. It is not mentioned in the early directories because they only cover Bodmin town not Bodmin Borough.

The keeper was recorded as Climo (1831) and in the Tithe (1840) the landowner was John Nicholls, the occupier was Joseph Hugo and the lessee was Mary Ann Climo beer seller & innkeeper. She died in 1858, aged 69. Later innkeepers included: Henry Holmes (1861), innkeeper and Chelsea Pensioner; William Best (1871 & 1873); James Greenway (1883 & 1889); Brunswick F J Whiting (1891-1897); Thomas Trethewey (1902); John Butler (1906–1910); his widow, Mary A Butler (until after 1923 - she died in 1934) and Henry Raymond Caswell (1935 until after 1939).

The **Borough Arms** is situated one mile from Bodmin on the Bodmin to Wadebridge road. It is still a popular public house today.

The 'Borough Arms' (1950s)
(Before the level of the car-park was raised)

The keepers, John & Mary Butler in front of the 'Borough Arms' (1904)

Cornish Arms (Plot 740)

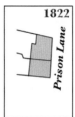
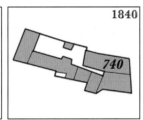
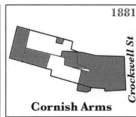
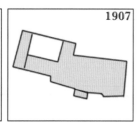

Douch reports that the **Cornish Arms** also known as the **Fifteen Balls** dated from 1773 and that the early innkeepers were Popham, Menhinnick and Pearse.[11] William Menhinnick appears in the 1791 Directory as Victualler with no associated hotel or inn.

In 1822/4 the address was 17, Prison Lane and the keeper Josias Spry, an ex member of the Cornwall Militia, Truro. Josias died in 1837 and his wife, Mary died in 1850. After 1844 John Bate was keeper, he was succeeded by John Carhart from 1856 to his death in 1868, followed by Edward James Levers (1868 to May 1886) when the licence was transferred to Thomas Butler. Further licence changes were: June 1894 transfer from Butler to Arthur Dobson Scroggie; September 1898 renewal of licence for

Cornish Arms by Sandoe & Son of the '*Royal Hotel*'. As Sandoe sold the '*Royal Hotel*' around 1900, it is not clear if later names are owners or managers. The list includes: Joseph Crispin Willis (1901 to after 1823); F W Wilmott (pre1935 to post1937) and Mrs Mabel Webber (1939).

The left-hand image shows the building jutting into the road before the 1980s rebuild. The **Cornish Arms** closed. The building was later demolished (ca. 2004).

Dog / Talbot Inn (Plot 325)

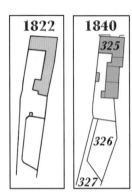

In 1787, when Arthur Jose took a lease on this inn on Fore Street, it was known as **The Dog**. This name was retained during the 1790s but when Francis Vincent took it over in 1807 it was changed to **The Talbot**.[12]

From before 1822 to 1839 the innkeeper was William Clyma. The Tithe map (1840) reports the landowner as the Hon. Anna Maria Agar and the new occupier was Alexander Bray. He died in 1851 and was replaced by Stephen Luxon, who was previously the innkeeper of the *Western Inn* which was also owned by the Lanhydrock family. Luxon died in December 1861 and the inn was closed. This was the third Robartes family Bodmin inn to be closed.

Site of Inn (2012): 54 & 56, Fore Street.

Exeter Inn (Plot 548)

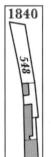

Francis Coleman was the keeper of the **Exeter** in the 1790s. In 1822-4 the address was 55, Bore Street and it was occupied by William Cocking. From 1827 the keeper & Landowner was John Davis until 1841. He was followed by William Warne (1844), F W Brokenshire (1847) and Richard Goss (1851-post1861).

The Inn closed after 1861 but Richard Goss and Family were still resident. His occupation had changed in 1871 to Grocer & Farmer. He died in 1874, aged 71. *Site of Inn (2012): 47, Higher Bore Street ('Exeter House').*

Fountain Inn (Plot 125)

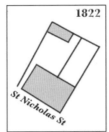 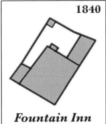 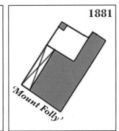

The **Fountain Inn** was owned by John Pascoe and occupied in 1822-4 by J Perry. Later innkeepers recorded are Thomas Harris (1830-1851); Richard Stephens (1852 until after 1861) and Samuel Hender (pre1871 to 1887).

Magistrates' records[8] show some very strange events occurring at this inn. In September 1887 the inn was allowed to open on Sundays for the first time. The next month Hender transferred the licence to James Sturridge, who tried to transfer it to Mrs Annie Blewitt (Mar. 1888) and to Mrs Q, Bennett (Apr. 1888). These were refused. In May 1888, Sturridge tried a transfer to Charles Bennett which was later granted. Charles Bennett transferred the licence to George Green in December 1888 and he tried to transfer to Joseph Nicholls (March 1889). This was refused as Joseph Nicholls *'was fined 40/- for keeping his house open during prohibited hours and was also fined 40/- at for selling Gin diluted with water.'* In May 1889 Green finally transferred the licence to Alfred Ernest Lean but the Inn was closed shortly after.

Fox / White Hart / Barley Sheaf (Plot 377)

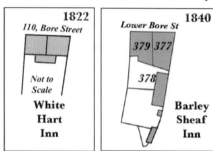

There is a document, dated 1741, indicating that this plot was an inn with the owner John Lewis, Innkeeper. He retired in 1765 and was succeeded by George Evans, Robert Pape, Thomas Hawken and James Wynn.[9]

Between 1765 and 1780 there are several Quarter Sessions records stating that 'the adjourned sessions were held at the **White Hart**, Bodmin.' In 1791 this was one of the two coaching inns in Bodmin and was recorded as **Pape's**. A sale document (1815) states: *Part of the late 'White Hart' previously called 'The Fox', occupied by Falmouth Mail Coach proprietors with stabling for 18 horses and garden; sold to James Wynn of Falmouth for £370; house late occupied by Mr Hawken, Mercer.*[9] This seems to be the end of the coaching business. The posting business was transferred from the **White Hart** to *Joll's Hotel* in 1806 when John Jewell moved to the hotel.

The 1822 street plan shows the position of the inn at 110, Bore Street. Later keepers included: William Crabb (1823/4), Robert Crabb (1830) and Brokenshire (1831).

A document dated March 1833 confirms the closure of this business. It states: *Dwelling house with yard & garden heretofore used as an inn/public house known as the 'White Hart' formerly in occupation of Wm. Jackson, late of Jn. Jewell, now of Jn. Wallis.*[9]

The **Barley Shea**f is first mentioned in 1839, the landowner was William Cornish and the keeper William Hoskin Whiting, listed as Butcher. Whiting remained as keeper until after 1871 when his daughter Mary became keeper (1873). He died in 1878 aged 77.

The next keeper was John Hawken until October 1886, when the police stated '*Mr Hawken is not a fit person to hold a licence in consequence of his being often drunk himself and causing rows and disturbances with his own family and permitting drunkenness by other people.*'[8] The Bench agreed but granted renewal on condition that an application for transfer would be made at the next special licensing meeting. The licence was transferred to Charlotte Jane Whiting, the eldest daughter of the late William Hoskin Whiting and sister of Mary Whiting. John Hawken was found guilty of being drunk and disorderly in the **Barley Sheaf** a few weeks after he lost the licence. He was fined 5/- with 8/6 costs.[8] In April 1889, Charlotte had the licence transferred to Mrs Mary Hawken, who remained keeper until about 1900. The inn was sold to St Austell Brewery in 1898 for £1,000. It was described as *having nine bedrooms, stabling for 40 horses, cart sheds and spacious lofts*.

Other innkeepers or managers recorded include: Edward Johnston (1902-1914); Walter Bound (1923-4); John M Wall, DSM and Violet Wall (1935-47). In 1939 the name had changed to the **Barley Sheaf** Hotel. It closed its doors in 2011.

Garland Ox (Plot 537)

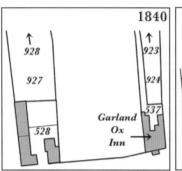
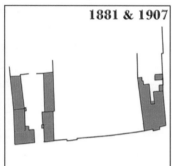

This Inn was built about 1820 on its present site. In 1822 it is shown as 63, Bore Street and is the last building on the Northern side of 'Bore Street'. The keeper was James Hayward (1823). William Solomon was Innkeeper from before 1830 to his death in 1841, when his wife Ann took over. The **Garland Ox** at this time consisted of six properties, **Garland Ox Inn** (537), Buildings & Courtlage (528), Garden (924) and three Meadows (923, 927 & 928). About 1846, Ann retired to a house in Fore Street and the new keeper was Thomas Richards, who died in 1855.

From 1856 until its sale in 1895, the inn was owned by the Hayes family. Samuel Bray Hayes, was described at different times as Victualler (1861), Inn Keeper (1871 & 1881) and Hay & Straw Dealer (1873 & 1883). He died in 1885 and the licence was transferred to his son William Grylls Hayes, Accountant and Deputy Registrar. He sold the property by Public Auction on the 20th April 1895 and died a few months later, aged 41.[8]

After 1895 the list of Keepers includes: Charles Keat (1897), Felix Ward (1901 & 1902); Thomas Bott (1906); Richard Henry Udy (1910-1918); Mrs Rhoda Udy (1919); Henry Albert Lingwood (1923); Bertram Marshall (1935) and H.T. Keith-Gillon (1939). After 1912 the establishment was known as the **Garland Ox Public House**.

The **Garland Ox** seems to be the only public house, still present in Bodmin, which has provided continuous service on the same site since about 1820.

George & Dragon (Plot 229)

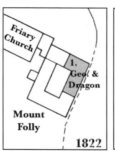 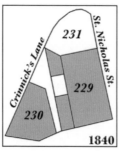  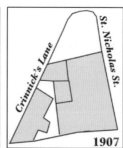

A tavern called the **The George** was recorded in a document of 1478 when William Worcestre visited the Friary. It seems unlikely that this inn lasted over 300 years to become the **George & Dragon**.

The **George & Dragon** was not mentioned in the 1791 Directory but it is shown on the 1822 town plan as part of the Friary buildings on Mount Folly. The Innkeeper was William Cavell (1823-4 Pigot's Directory). This position of the Inn was confirmed in the 1831 Census: Cavell (214) occupied the **George & Dragon** and Marshall (212) & Bonady (213) lived in the adjacent properties. In 1830 the innkeeper was Julia Cavell. By 1840 the inn had moved to its present location, plot 229 on the Tithe Map. The original building, being part of the Friary was demolished around 1836 to make space for the new Assize Court building. The landowner and Occupier is listed as Henry Bonady. Julia Cavell and her son William were listed as the landowner & occupier of the *Eight Bells* in Castle Street but Julia Cavell returned to the **George & Dragon** in 1841. Henry Bonady was the occupier in 1844 but he sold the inn together with the brew-house and large stable and the adjacent house to William Levers in January, 1847. This article in the '*West Britain*' also states that the business had been carried on for over fifty years. (This suggests that the original **George & Dragon** was opened in the early 1790s). The lease on the dwelling house had run for ten years in 1846. From this information it would seem that the inn and the adjacent house were

newly built in 1836. This is consistent with the demolition of the old building on Mount Folly. William Levers continued as keeper (1847 & 1861) and was succeeded by Matthew Doney (1871 & 1873).

The entry in the 1881 census is quite complicated and includes: Thomas Brock, Head, M, 33, Carpenter & Innkeeper; Jane Brock, Wife, 34; Ellen Tamblyn, Stepdaughter, 8 and William Levers, W, 79, Formerly Innkeeper. Further research shows that Jane Hawke Levers, daughter of William Levers, was married to Petherick Tamblyn (Bodmin 1868). He died in 1873 aged 33 and she later married Thomas Brock (1878). The Inn was still in the hands of the Levers family until the transfer of the licence in November 1889. William Levers died in 1890 aged 90, Jane Hawke Brock died in 1894, aged 49 and Thomas Brock died in 1895, aged 47.

From November 1889 until after 1914, the innkeeper was Mrs Ann H Day, who died in Bodmin in 1919. In 1923 the occupier was Ambrose Matthews and in 1935-39 it was Arthur Basil Holden.

This inn is still in business.

Family History Notes [4]

Bonady Family:

Several early documents contain the name Henry Bonady. Was this a unique individual or several related people? A search of Parish Records and Census Returns suggests that there were three generations with the same name.

Henry Bonady (1) (1779-1838), Cordwainer, son of William Bonady and Elizabeth;

Henry Bonady (2) (1805-1881), Cordwainer, son of Henry(1) and Jenifer Ley and

Henry Bonady(3) (born 1833), Cordwainer, son of Henry(2) and Sarah.

Only Henry's (1) & (2) were involved in the running of the *'George & Dragon'*.

Cavell Family:

This family was involved in running the *'George & Dragon'* and the *'Eight Bells'*.

William Cavell (Born: ca.1780) married Julia Bate (Born: ca.1783) in Bodmin (1810).

They had three sons William (B: 1813), Thomas Bate (B: 1815) and John (B: 1818).

The story of this family involves the high death rate. William, the innkeeper of the first *'George & Dragon'* died in 1826, aged 33 and Julia became innkeeper. John died in 1835, aged 17 and Thomas Bate died in 1840, aged 24.

In 1840 Julia was listed as landowner of the *'Eight Bells'* and her son William was the occupier.

In the next year, Julia had returned to the *'George & Dragon'* and the *'Eight Bells'* had a new innkeeper. William is listed at the *'Eight Bells'* in 1844 & 1847. Julia died in 1846, aged 63 and William died in 1847 aged 33. This was the end of the *'Eight Bells Inn'* and this family of innkeepers.

The Globe (Plot 107)

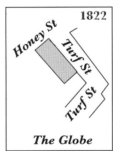
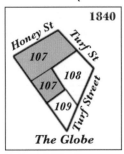

This inn was first reported in the 1820s, at 6, Honey Street with keeper Joseph Kent. The next occupant, William Fiddick, is listed as innkeeper from before 1830 until his death in 1867 aged 83. He was followed by Thomas Baron (1867-post1873) then William Bartlett until his death in 1889 aged 66. The licence was transferred to his wife Kezia. In 1895, Samuel William Jewell applied to the Magistrates to transfer the licence to his wife, Elizabeth Ann Jewell, this request was refused. William S May was the innkeeper from about 1901 until **The Globe** closed (between 1906-1910).

The owner at this time was Redruth Brewey Ltd., and the building was used as a central store for their Wine & Spirit Business. This facility had been moved from the premises, later called the *'Hole in the Wall'* in Crockwell Street. This brewery was taken over by Devonish in 1934 and by 1939 **The Globe** was re-opened with Charles E Jackson as manager.

In 1959, the name was changed to the **Duke of Cornwall** and the building was finally demolished for a road widening scheme in 1992.

©Cornish Studies Library (Ellis Collection)

The end of the Globe Inn
©Dudley Prout

Golden Lion / White Hart II (Plot 805)

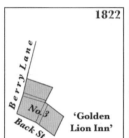 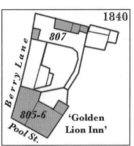  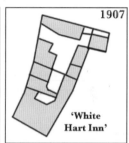

The **Golden Lion** first appears in 1822 at 3, Back Street. The landowner in 1840 was Richard Hocken. The innkeepers were James Dumble (1830), Harvey (1831) and James Bray (1839–1844). There is one further document (1847 Williams Commercial Directory) which mentions the **Golden Lion** but it gives the address as Honey Street, the keeper as John Warne, who was keeper of the *Omnibus & Railway Inn* at this time. It would appear that this inn closed down in the late 1840s or early 1850s.

In 1852/3 this plot was occupied by a new **White Hart Inn**. The innkeepers were John Hawey (1852/3) and John Ough (1856). From before 1861 the house was taken over by three generations of the Verran Family: Walter Verran (1861-1871); Walter junior (1871-1885); Walter's Widow, Ellen (1885-1901) and Walter & Ellen's son, Walter Thomas (1902 until his death in 1915). Later occupiers include Mrs Mary Emily Thomas (1923 & 1935) and Mrs Dorothy Winifred Watson (1939).

The **White Hart Inn** is still open for business.

Kings Arms / Royal Hotel (Plot 706)

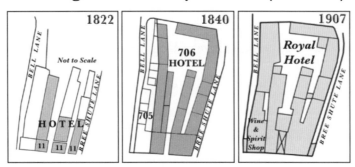

The maps show that the footprint of the buildings did not change significantly over the years. The main change was the incorporation of plot 705 into the Hotel site. This property was owned by Thos. Clarke, Druggist & Chemist from before 1831. His son Thomas Taunton Clarke, Druggist & Coal Merchant, sold the buildings to the Hotel after 1881.

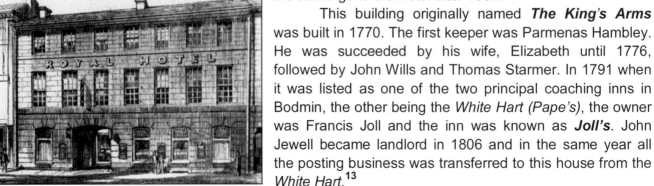

This building originally named **The King's Arms** was built in 1770. The first keeper was Parmenas Hambley. He was succeeded by his wife, Elizabeth until 1776, followed by John Wills and Thomas Starmer. In 1791 when it was listed as one of the two principal coaching inns in Bodmin, the other being the *White Hart (Pape's)*, the owner was Francis Joll and the inn was known as **Joll's**. John Jewell became landlord in 1806 and in the same year all the posting business was transferred to this house from the *White Hart*.[13]

The next proprietor was Richard Oliver and the business was known as **Oliver's Hotel**. He died in 1830 and was followed by his son, William. In 1847, he was appointed posting master at Bodmin to the Establishment of Her Majesty's Stables. By 1856 the name of the hotel was changed to **Oliver's Royal Hotel**.

Before 1871, Augustus Coombe Sandoe, born about 1821 in St Blazey and who had previously been the Innkeeper at the *Town Arms* (1861) became the new proprietor. In 1885 the licence was transferred into the names of A C Sandoe and W A Sandoe. The business was expanded with the opening of a Wine & Spirit merchant *'Sandoe & Son'* on the adjacent plot (705). He sold the **Royal Hotel** together with the Wine Merchants in 1900 when he retired (age about 80). In the 1901 census A C Sandoe was listed as Farmer and his son, William Augustus, was listed as Retired Wine Merchant (age 37!!).

Both businesses were sold to D Rolinson, who renamed the wine merchants. Later owners included Isaac Lake (pre1914 to 1923); C & R Reed (1935) and Kayes (Kingsbridge) Ltd (1939) used the name *A C Sandoe & Son* for the Wine Merchants. H R Franklin was proprietor and Mrs D M Poland, Manageress in 1947.

In 1949 the landlord, W E Milton Ayers, registered his company as **Royal Hotel (Bodmin) Ltd**.[14] In the documentation is a detailed description of the business: *The **Royal Hotel**, Bodmin has 25 bedrooms and carries on the business of hotel, restaurant, cafe tavern, wine, beer and spirit merchants, caterers for public amusements generally, proprietors of motor and other vehicles etc. Mr Avery agreed that references to 'brewers, maltsters, distillers, importers and manufacturers of aerated mineral and* *artificial waters'* should be deleted from the principal objects of the new company. The hotel is the principal hotel in Bodmin - it is on the main A30 road from London through Cornwall. It has an estimated turnover of £25,000 for the next 12 months.

Although the building was listed as '*of Special Architectural or Historic Interest*' the contents of hotel were sold by auction in 1968 and it was demolished. The new building contained the original stone frontage on the 1st & 2nd floors.

The two-storey building on the left of image replaced the original four-storey Wine & Spirits Merchants.

King's Arms Inn (Plot 702)

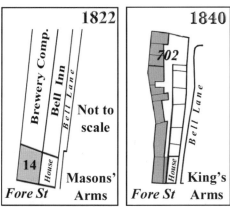

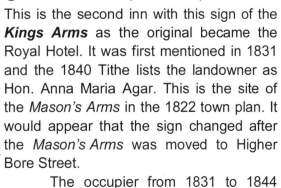

This is the second inn with this sign of the **Kings Arms** as the original became the Royal Hotel. It was first mentioned in 1831 and the 1840 Tithe lists the landowner as Hon. Anna Maria Agar. This is the site of the *Mason's Arms* in the 1822 town plan. It would appear that the sign changed after the *Mason's Arms* was moved to Higher Bore Street.

The occupier from 1831 to 1844 was John Collins. He died in 1847, aged 67, and was succeeded by James Cock (1847) and John Ough (1852/3). This establishment closed shortly after this entry. This was the second Bodmin inn owned by the Robartes family to close.

Site of inn (2012): 29 Fore St which is now part of Dorothy Perkins & Millet's buildings.

A Directory of 1791 describes the transport and communications systems between Bodmin and the outside world in the late eighteen century

"A stage-coach has been set up, which runs from Falmouth to Exeter in two days. It stops at this place (Bodmin) Monday, Wednesday and Friday; dines going to Exeter and sleeps going back. The principal inns are the White Hart (Pape's) and the King's Arms (Joll's). There is a waggon from Exeter and Plymouth every Monday, which returns the next day.

The post-office opens at eight o'clock in the morning and shuts at ten in the evening. The mail is conveyed from Exeter on horseback and sometimes in a cart."

London Inn (Plot 101)

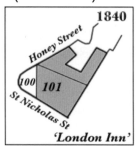

This inn appears in the 1791 document, keeper George Wells. In the early 1820s the address is 1, Honey St or St Nicholas Street, depending on the document, and the keeper was R. Wells. He was succeeded by Joseph Kent (1830-1) and Peter Paul Couch (1839). The Tithe (1840) shows the owner as the Honourable Anna Maria Agar and the Occupier as Wm. Willcock, who died in 1843. The new occupier was Mary Ann Kent (until after 1853). The last occupier was John May.

The building was demolished in 1871 and a new building was erected on the site in 1872. The **London Inn** was the last of the four Bodmin inns owned by the Robartes family of Lanhydrock to be closed. *Site of Inn (2012): Turret House, Mount Folly.*

Mason's Arms

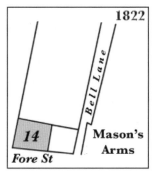 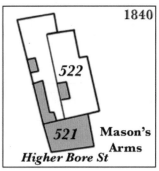 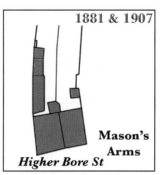

The **Mason's Arms** is shown on the 1822 town plan as the second building west of Bell Lane in Fore Street. The *innkeeper* was William Collins.

Before 1831 it had moved to a new site in Higher Bore Street, west of the *Garland Ox*, under the management of Samuel Tabb, *Mason* and *Beer Seller*. (This plot corresponds to No.83 Higher Bore Street).

In the early 1840s, Samuel Tabb transferred the **Mason's Arms** to William Harvey, *Carpenter* (*and Beer Seller in the 1831 Census*), who lived in a property in Higher Bore Street near the top of Bore Lane, the site of the present **Mason's Arms**, address 5-7, Higher Bore Street. Samuel Tabb continued living in the original building and died there in 1888, aged 90.

In the census of 1851, Wm. Harvey is listed as *Innkeeper* and in 1861 as *Carpenter* and *Beer House Keeper*. He died in 1870, aged 85 and was succeeded by Jane Murray, *Beer House Keeper* (1871). Before 1881 the Britt family had taken over the premises: 1881, Betsy Parry Britt, (died 1888: age 42) was followed by her husband William Rees Britt and his second wife Elizabeth Ann (Census 1891). In

August 1900, the Magistrates transferred the licence from William Rees Britt to Henry Titball, *Beer Retailer*. He still had the licence in 1939 and he died in 1945, aged 92.

This business was rarely listed in Directories under *'Inns & Hotels'* or even **'Mason's Arms'**. The names and dates were found in the Commercial Sections under Beer Retailers/Sellers.

It would appear that Wallis (1831) was correct to list the **Mason's Arms** as a Beer House and not an Inn. Although beer houses were generally short lived businesses the **Mason's Arms** seems to be the exception in that it has lasted for around 200 years and is still open today.

Miners Arms, St Lawrence

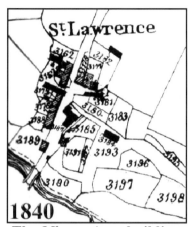

The *Miners Arms* building has not been identified.

St Lawrence is a small village about 1.5 miles South West of Bodmin on the southern edge of the parish. It was the site of St Lawrence's Leper Hospital.

The earliest record found for the inn is a lease between Lord & Lady Grenville and Simon Merifield dated 1819 for *'all that tenement known by the name of the **Miners Arms** public house situate at St Lawrence in the Parish of Bodmin'.* [15]

In 1831 it was called the **Miners Inn** and the keeper was Merrifield. There are no entries for the Miners in the Tithe (1840) or the Census (1841). Again in 1851, the inn is not mentioned but William Clyma is listed as Innkeeper.

The **Miners Arms** is listed in two directories from the 1850s and the 1861 Census. The innkeeper in these three documents is James Lobb. He died in the Miners Inn, St Lawrence on the 10th November, 1865. No more reports on this inn have been found.

Image of the *Miners Arms* shortly before the inn closed. (1864)

The New Inn

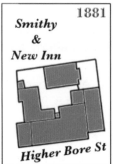
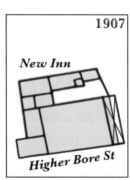

In 1822 **The New Inn** was situated in Fore Street between the *Town Arms* and Carriers Lane. The keeper was John Hoskins.

In the 1831 Census the Innkeeper was Stephens. He was replaced by Samuel Crabb before the end of the year and he continued until 1839. The Tithe data clearly shows that the **New Inn**, occupied by the owner, Nicholas Stevens, is still situated in Fore Street but in 1841 Nicholas Stephens is listed as Yeoman and the **New Inn** is not named.

The next mention of the inn is in 1856 when the address was Bore Street and the owner was Richard Wendon. He was a blacksmith and had lived in Bore Street since before 1840 (plot 513). Before 1861 he described himself as Blacksmith & Beer House Keeper and the

THE NEW INN
BODMIN

BED AND BREAKFAST

PLAIN AND FANCY TEAS

Excellent Accommodation for Tourists

H. MARTIN, *Proprietor*

building as the **New Inn**. He died in 1874, aged 75. His son described his occupation as Blacksmith and Publican (1881).

After 1881 there were quite a number of keepers: Mary Lawry (1883-5, Beer Retailer); John Harfoot (1889, Beer Retailer); John Matthews (1891, Publican); Robert Cartwright (1893 & 1897); George Hawke (1901-1911, Tailor and Beer Seller); Arthur Clarke (1914, Beer Retailer); John Mitchell, 1923, (Beer Retailer) and H. Martin (Proprietor).

In the 1930s, the name was changed to **The New Inn Hotel**, proprietors, Jos. M. McGregor (1935) and Cyril Arscott Webber (1939). The business was now aimed at tourism as judged by the 1920s advertisement.

The original Inn in Fore St which closed after 1840 was resurrected as a Beer House in Higher Bore Street (later number 1, St Leonards). Since 1856, this business has been on the same site. The building is now the **Cat & Fiddle** Pub and Restaurant.

Omnibus Inn (Plot 786)

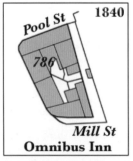

Appproximate position of the 'Omnibus/Railway Inn'

First mentioned in directories in 1839 as the **Omnibus & Railway Inn** it was also listed in 1840 as the **Omnibus Inn**. The landowner was Thomas Clarke and the address was Pool Street / Back Street.

The keepers were Chris Mules (1839), William Levers (1840), John Warne (from before 1847 until his death in 1867) and his widow, Elizabeth (until 1872) and finally James Heal in 1873.

From 1850 it was called the **Railway Inn** or **Railway Arms Inn**. It closed after 1873 and there seems to have been changes within the footprint of the plot.

Red Lion Inn (Plot 335)

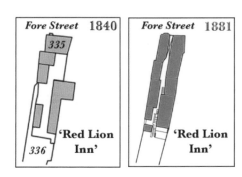

First recorded at 57, Fore Street in 1822. The first innkeepers were Stephen Pascoe who died in 1827 and his wife Elizabeth (died 1838). From 1839 the landowner was Polkinghorne with Richard Dodge Phillips and Katherine as keepers. Richard died in 1846, aged 39 and his wife continued for a short time.

From before 1851, John May was innkeeper until he retired at 70 (1881) and was succeeded by Edward Tank who transferred the licence to James Brenton in December 1888. Brenton died in 1889, aged 33 and the licence was transferred to Mrs Hannah Jane Brenton (September 1889). In January 1890 Mrs Brenton tried to transfer the licence to Charles Bennett but Sergeant Vercoe *'objected to the manner in which Bennett had run the 'Fountain' and that Mr Bennett was not a fitting person to hold the licence.'* The transfer was refused.[8]

However in the same month the police visited the **Red Lion** and found that Mrs Brenton did not live there and rarely visited. The Inn was being run by the same Charles Bennett and his family!

In September 1890 an application for renewal of the licence by Mrs Brenton was refused.[8] This resulted in the closure of the **Red Lion**.

Site of inn (2012): 60-62 Fore Street (Woolacotts).

St. Petroc's Hotel (Plot 205)

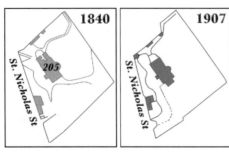

In 1831 this large regency house was the property of John Wallis, Solicitor. In the tithe the landowner and occupier was Louisa Sarel, wife of Andrew Lovering Sarel of Grove House Enfield.

John Wallis died in April 1842 and Sarel, one of his executors died in April 1843. This led, over several years to a number of complex legal cases involving members of the Wallis family and the Sarels. (Details are available in the Malcolm McCarthy Collection[8].) By 1851 the occupier was Preston Wallis, Solicitor, son of John Wallis. He died in 1858 and his widow and family were still in the house in 1871. Later occupiers were John Hitchins, J.P., (1881) and Harry Y Jamieson, Magistrate, in 1891. In 1901 the house became **St. Petroc's Private Hotel** with Samuel W Jewell as owner. He died in 1913, aged 62. There are no entries for this hotel in the 1914 and 1923 directories.

From 1924 until after 1939 the Private Hotel reappeared with owners C & R Reed and proprietors W E & P L Bolt. In a 1947 Bodmin Guide there is an advertisement for **St. Petroc's Hotel & Club** but no mention of the owners or proprietors. The hotel became a Care Home in the late 1980s.

The Tavern/Turks Head/Queen's Head Inn/Hotel (Plot 251-2)

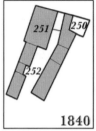   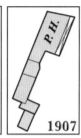

The earliest mention of this building is in a rent roll of 1747 when the tenant was William Marshall. **The Tavern** was the principal inn of Bodmin at that time.[16] There are a number of leases for this property held at the CRO. Lease from Thomas Pitt to T W Partington of London, *dwelling house called* **'Turks Head'** *in Fore Street, Bodmin* (1756); lease from Thos. Pitt to Thos. Hawken of Bodmin, *dwelling etc. commonly called heretofore* **'Turks Head'** *now* **'Queens Head'***, where Chas. Rounsevell then Henry May and lately William Marshall dwelt, now occupied by Thos. Hawken* (1767). In 1768, Hawken closed the inn and moved to the *'White Hart'*. There is a further lease (1784) *from Lord Camelford to John Eyre, St Mabyn,* and a sale document; John Eyre of Kenwyn, Merchant, to Richard Long of Bodmin, Hairdresser, *several properties including a house formerly called the* **'Turks Head'** *lately the* **'Queens Head'** (1814).

This inn is not mentioned in the 1790s lists but in 1822 the address was 83, Fore Street and the occupier was Robert Crabb. From 1830 to 1841, the keeper was James Coul and from 1840-47 the occupier was Thomas Tabb.

This establishment had a large number of keepers including; Thomas Harris (1851-6); Elizabeth Frampton (1861); Andrew Seale (1871-6) and his Widow, Emma (1876-1885); Edward Albert Grove (1885-July 1886); John Peter Billing (July 1886-post 1906); Charles Merrifield (1910-14); John Brown (1923); Stanley Harwood Davies (1935) and Charles Harold Tyler (1939). A Bodmin Guide of 1937 states the owner of the **Queen's Head Hotel** as Plymouth Brewery Ltd.

This hotel closed in 1984, the building was demolished in Feb.1986 and rebuilt in 1987, retaining the conserved 'red brick' facade.

Town Arms (Plot 693)

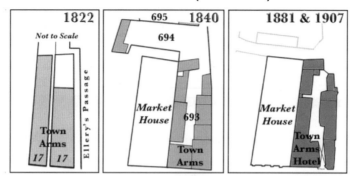

The **Town Arms** first appeared on the 1822 town plan at 17, Fore Street, on the west side of Ellery's Passage. In 1840 it was in the same place but it was now adjacent to the new market hall.

In addition to plot 693 the landowner, Gatty, also owned plots 694 & 695. It seems that after 1840 these additional plots were developed to give new buildings and a roadway from Market Street to Bell Lane. There was also rebuilding on the main plot. The first keeper was also the owner, Thomas Gatty (1761-1825). On his death the inn was transferred to his son, Robert who died in 1848 aged 45. The next innkeeper was John Frampton, previously Bailiff of Glyn Farm, Cardinham, who died in 1852, aged 46. His widow Elizabeth, continued until after 1856. Augustus Coombe Sandoe, later owner of the *Royal Hotel*, was in occupation in 1861.

In the 1870s and 1880s there were major changes to this house. In 1871 the name changed to the **Town Arms Hotel** and the occupier was Wm. Lobb, innkeeper. From 1881 to before 1889 the occupier was Charles Crabb, Manager and Managing Director of the company '***Town Arms Family & Commercial Hotel Co., Ltd.***'.

The later proprietors/managers were Nicholas Robins (1889-1897); John Prisk (1889); Charles

41

Lean (1897); E K Brierley (1902); Joseph James Winn (1906-1910); Thomas Robert Hards (1914); John Evelyn Hill (1923); St Austell Brewery (1935), and finally Walter Hicks & Co., Ltd. (*St Austell Brewery*) in 1937. The Hotel was closed before 1939.

L E Long reports that there was great rivalry between the *Royal Hotel* and the **Town Arms Hotel** on several levels. Not only did their busses race each other to collect customers from Bodmin Road station but rival opposing factions of the Town Council used the two hotels. The Liberals were based at the **Town Arms** and the Conservatives the *Royal*.

However there are a number of documents, showing that before 1913 the two establishments were united in a business called *Royal Hotel* & **Town Arms** *Livery Stables*. The company rented horses, carriages, cars, hearses and was a mail contractor. It claimed omnibuses meet all G.W. trains. It would seem by this time the earlier rivalry had been forgotten.

The two images on the next page are dated 1920 and 2010. The windows and the cartouche, which held the name **'Town Arms Hotel'** are identical in both pictures. Only the ground floor has been changed. In the modern image the dark area bottom right is *'Ellery's Passage'* now known as *'Town Arms Passage'*.

Union Inn (Plot 732-3)

In 1822 the **Union Inn** was listed at 5, Prison Lane, with Francis Bligh as innkeeper. He was still owner in 1831. From 1839 to 1844 the landowner/keeper was John Moody. The last entry for this inn is in 1847 with the owner listed as Richard Pearse. The status of this establishment is in some doubt. In addition to being called **Union Inn** it was listed as 'House & Garden' (1840) and **Union Hotel** in 1830. *Site of inn (2012): Piazza (part) formerly 7-9 Crockwell Street.*

Western Inn (Plots 390-1)

The earliest reference to the **Western Inn** is in 1822-4 when it was listed as 106, Fore Street and the innkeeper was Stephen Luxon. In the tithe the landowner was listed as the Hon. Anna Maria Agar of Lanhydrock. When Luxon moved to *The Talbot* in 1851 this establishment was closed. This was the first Lanhydrock owned inn to be closed. The buildings were then occupied by Simon Hugo, grocer and *Temperance Hotel* owner. After his death in 1879 his son Frederick continued until the building was demolished to make way for the library in 1896.

Other Inns and Beer Houses

The following Table contains establishments for which no further information has been found.

Sign	Date	Innkeeper	Comment	Reference.
Bear	1791	Wm. Marshall		1791 Directory
Ship	1784	Wm. Sloggett	South side of Fore Street	*Douch,* page 196
	1791	Wm. Davy		1791 Directory
The Star	1791	Walter Spry		1791 Directory
Rose & Crown	1761	Marshall Family	Transfer from Wm. to L. Marshall	*Douch,* page 94
The Grapes	1775-76	John Wills	Keeper moved to Kings Arms	*Douch,* page 205
Three Cranes	18th Century		No further information	*Douch,* page 204
Maltster's Arms	18th Century		No further information	*Douch,* page 204
The Sun	18th Century		Rowlandson image ca. 1800	*Douch,* page 128
Waggoners Arms			No further information	*Douch,* page 189
Race-Course Inn	1814		Racecourse Farm, Bodmin Downs	*Douch,* page 166
William IV	1831	Parnall	St Nicholas St	Census No. 225
Pack Horse	1831	Dumble	Pool St	Census No.305
Miner's Arms	1831	Harper	Higher Bore St. Closed late 1831	Census No.663
Beer House	1831	Colly	Prison Lane. Closed late 1831	Census no.379
Beer House	1831	Hayes	Lower Bore St	Census No.545
Beer House	1831	Harris	Lower Bore St. Opened late 1831	Census No.566
The Crispin	1791-1820?	Elizabeth Lean	Higher Bore St. Ruin in 1831	Census No.638-9
Spry's Arms	1840	J. Williams	Modern Address: 24, Lower Bore St.	Tithe Map (402)
Wheaten Sheaf	1845? -1875		No further information	*Douch,* page 187

Number of Inns/Hotels in Bodmin

'*The Universal Directory of Great Britain 1791*', published on CD by *Archivebooks.org* contains a list of Bodmin traders including the following Innkeepers: **London Inn** (George Wells); **King's Arms** (Francis Joll); **White Hart** (Robert Pape) and the **Exeter Inn** (Francis Coleman) and Victuallers: **Bear** (William Marshall); **Ship**, (William Davy); **Blue Hart** (Thomas Bate); **The Star** (Walter Spry); **Bell Inn** (Mary Ann Carpenter); **The Dog** (Arthur Jose); **The Crispin** (Elizabeth Lean) and five others with no associated inn. This suggests that there were between 11 and 16 inns in Bodmin at this time.

In the early 1820s, 19,^{3} and 20,^{5} inns are listed. Wallis (1831 Census) lists 22, including St Lawrence and Dunmeer and 7 beer houses. The tithe (1840) lists 25 establishments. This is a large number for a Borough with the population of ca.4500 people. This seems to be the high point for inns in Bodmin as after the Tithe there is a marked decline in numbers. By 1871 there were only 15 inns/hotels and this fell to an average of 11-12 during the whole of the 20th century. In 2000 there were 12 pubs/hotels. Since then the **Cornish Arms** and the **Barley Sheaf** have closed but the **Chapel an Gansblydhen** (J D Wetherspoon) and two hotels have opened.

It is not possible to explain the closure of many of these properties but in some cases the reasons seem clear:

In 1840 four inns in Bodmin were owned by Hon. Anna Maria Agar, member of the Robartes family of Lanhydrock. Between 1848 and 1871 these inns together with the **White Hart** of Lanhydrock were closed. This would seem to be a deliberate policy of the family to move away from inn ownership.

Later in the 19th century the magistrates were more critical of innkeepers and were very careful when issuing licences. Many transfers were refused because the applicants '*were not suitable persons to run an inn*'. This issue led directly to the closure of both **The Fountain** and the **Red Lion**.

Some of the inns and hotels must have closed for commercial reasons and **The Globe/Duke of Cornwall** was demolished for a road widening scheme.

Index

Barley Sheaf	16	Garland Ox	18	Oliver's Hotel	27	St Petroc's Hotel	38
Bear, The	45	George & Dragon	20	Oliver's Royal Hotel	27	*Star, The*	45
Bell Inn	8	Globe, The	23	Omnibus & Railway	36	*Sun, The*	45
Blue Hart	9	Golden Lion	25	Omnibus Inn	36	Talbot Inn	14
Board, The	10	*Grapes, The*	45	Pack Horse	45	Tavern, The	39
Borough Arms	12	Hole in the Wall	10	Pape's Hotel	16	*Three Cranes*	45
Borough Bounds	12	Jewell's Hotel	26	Queen's Head, The	39	Town Arms	41
Cat & Fiddle	35	Joll's Hotel	26	*Race-Course Inn*	45	Turks Head, The	39
Cornish Arms	13	King's Arms	26	Railway Arms Inn	36	Union Inn	44
Crispin, The	45	King's Arms II	29	Railway Inn	36	*Waggoners Arms*	45
Dog, The	14	London Inn	30	Red Lion Inn	37	Western Inn	44
Duke of Cornwall	23	*Maltster's Arms*	45	*Rose & Crown*	45	*Wheaten Sheaf*	45
Eight Bells	9	Masons Arms	31	Royal Hotel	26	White Hart	16
Exeter Inn	14	*Miner's Arms*	45	Sandoe's Royal Hotel	27	White Hart II	25
Fountain Inn	15	Miners' Arms/Inn	33	*Ship. The*	45	*William IV*	45
Fox, The	16	New Inn, The	34	*Spry's Arms*	45	*Italic= few details*	

Directory of Bodmin Inns & Hotels 2012

HOTELS	Address	Post Code	PUBS (continued)	Address	Post Code
Lanhydrock Hotel & Golf Club	Lanhydrock	PL30 5AQ	Chapel an Gansblydhen	Fore Street	PL31 2HR
Premier Inn	Launceston Rd	PL31 2RW	Garland Ox	Higher Bore St	PL31 1JS
Westberry Hotel	Rhind Street	PL31 2EL	George & Dragon	St Nicholas St	PL31 1AB
PUBS			Hole in the Wall	Crockwell St	Pl31 2DS
Bodmin Jail	Berrycoombe Rd	PL31 2NR	Masons Arms	Higher Bore St	PL31 1JS
Borough Arms	Dunmere	PL31 2RD	Weavers, The	Honey Street	PL31 2DL
Cat & Fiddle	St Leonards	PL31 1JZ	White Hart	Pool Street	PL31 2HA

References and Sources

1. Douch, H L in *'Old Cornish Inns'*. Pub: D Bradford Barton, 1966 (WHJ).
2. Long, L E in *'An Old Cornish Town'*. Pub: Bodmin Books, 1975 (WHJ)..
3. Directories: 1791, 1793-8, 1823-4, 1830, 1839, 1883, 1889, 1893, 1910, 1914, 1923, 1935, 1939. (WHJ). Other directories and dates: 1844, 1852-3, 1856, 1873, 1893, 1897, 1902, 1906 at *www.historicaldirectories.org.*, 1847 (Bodmin Town Museum).
4. Census Data: 1831: *'The Bodmin Register'* (Pub: 1827 to 1838) (WHJ); 1841-1891: Cornwall Online Census Project; 1901: *www.1901censusonline.com.* 1911: *www.1911census.co.uk*
5. Document Ref. RIC, MMP/22/1., Courtney Library, Truro.
6. Tithe Map and apportionment data. © WH & JM Johnson / Bodmin Town Museum.
7. Ordnance Survey maps 1881 & 1907: (Bodmin Town Museum).
8. Malcolm McCarthy Document Collection at *mccarthyindex.org*.
9. Cornwall Records Office. Search at *www.nationalarchives.gov.uk/a2a*. Copies of documents provided by Cornwall Records Office, Truro.
10. Bodmin Guardian March 13th, 1914, p2.
11. Douch, *reference 1,* page 144
12. Douch, *reference 1*, page 169
13. Douch, *reference 1,* page 95.
14. National Archive: Document Number: *HO 45/23888*.
15. Cornwall Records Office: Document F/4/200/15, dated 26th March 1819.
16. Maclean, John in *'Parochial and Family History of the Borough of Bodmin in the County of Cornwall',* 1870 (WHJ).